Paper Plague

Norma Mahns

DEDICATED TO THE PUBLIC

CONTENTS

Paper Plague

ACKNOWLEDGMENTS

The poem "Oppression" was originally published
by *Planet Roc* in 1979.

"Sepulcher" (edited) appeared in *Lumpen Times*, Premier Issue #7

"Wolkins" published, *Lumpen Times*, Issue #10, 1993

"Cold Moon" published by Chicago Poetry Press, 2017

"Uranium Butterfly" published by Veteran for Peace, 2017

Paper Plague

Preface

This chapbook is intended to be read in one to three sittings immediately consecutively, in order to obtain the whole experience, the author wishes the reader to feel. What is Paper Plague about? It is about an attitude toward life. It is about liberty, lamentation, and love. It is an awakening into an ultimate love. In his poem "Christ Climbed Down," Lawrence Ferlinghetti touched on the emotion with his line "the very craziest of Second Comings." This is what Paper Plague is about, the Second Coming, which comes in the form of liberation, repentance and love complete between man and woman, personally for the author. Some poems have a Freudian point of view, therefore, since Freud specialized in dreams and the sexual oppressions of man, these poems reach into the mind to reveal what it means to have libido – love/sex. This is one form of a rapture, according to the point of view incorporated in the body of this collection.

Two of the poems embody spontaneous dreams, (received during sleep). "Dream Call" is a visual poem which is about a child-an artist who collects an audience – a heavenly mission. We all have a mission, a gift. The poem is episodic. So hopefully there will be more to come connected to "Dream Call." The other visual poems "Babies Given Up," embodies the dream within its last two lines – "pray that it is not a pig who receives suck, while a mother gives milk." These words were from the dream of an artist friend. She saw a single breast giving a tiny pig suck (breast). The poem is also about modern day motherhood. If Christ asked her to stand on the other side of the fence from her children to represent the ultimate motherhood would she do it? The truest mother would. Therefore, the type of love which reaches revelation is a rarity for it is not only a love between man and woman, but woman's love of the world, to nurse it.

The poetry is philosophical, but not a new philosophy. Dante held this to be the divine truth – redemption is always obtainable, thus qualifying the believer for rapture. Therefore, the subject of politics cannot be avoided, for the humanitarian love of fellow citizen, and forgiveness of neighbor also bonds a man and woman's love to deep levels.

The poetry is political in the sense that it maintains the Revelations described in the New Testament is spiritual, and not in the least intended to be literal. Therefore, the poetry condemns war of the flesh. While it does advocate war of the spirit. It is a war to the dept of understanding the inner battle a generation must deal with in order to get along globally with citizens of the earth as well as getting along with each other at home. It is for a generation who demands the truth – highest love, and complete freedom to obtain uncompromising individuality. It is love between man and woman bonded by the spirit of Jesus, and God as the creative artist, while having knowledge of the man/woman conflicts that honestly exist.

The poetry in Paper Plague is deep; and, the delicate emotions can be missed if one does not have a kindred spirit to the emotions portrayed. There is no denying that the poems are on the idiosyncratic side. However, it is very readable for our times and the collection is intended to be a mere sharing of feelings – it is just poetry nothing more, so enjoy.

LIBERTY

O

    ppres

      s

      i

      o

      n

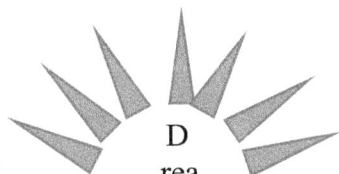

          I   D

                   rea

                   M

                   I

                 AM

                  a

                cock

                  a

                too

             perched

                on

                 a

               tree

          singing to the

             horses

            beneath

          the sea.

        But when I

      awake from this

    sweet liberty, I see

I am just a jester juggling infinitely for Liberty.

Woman

She is no goddess

Vanity is emptiness

Just a crazy mood

Flutters of Revelation

Like little butterflies
In our minds, one at a time
A flash must be catched, least lost
Never to be known, nor sown
By our delicate wings.
Vibrations metamorphosize into thought.
Scatters, shatters
The prince of the air
While it tames our keen minds.

JOE's Clone

A cure for every ache a clone alone

Will take the aches and pains for Joe he will be.

And so, Joe called the doctor on the phone

Complaining he had one damn aching head.

Doc said, "Don't fear, I have the cure for you!"

And Doc then promised Joe he'd send his clone.

Joe rested well with what the Doc had said.

Joe dreamt of flying a new golden kite.

Joe slept not with wife, only his clone.

To his clone Joe spoke words without fear.

When I must die will you take a fool's death?

For I will wish to live my life instead.

Joe's clone did smile and said, course Joe

Don't dread, I will take Joe dead.

It is Tax Day

I am lost, myself is swallowed in this void-

Black hole of this green machine.

Do you want my number to know who I am?

My fingerprints painted on the palms of my hand.

I am that number on your wall, on your shelf.

The real self is in hell with economic sores.

As you pretend to help the poor

We are alive only in your green machine.

The poor do not help; they were born simple, happy, laughing.

We pledge Patriotism, we pledge to Mother Country.

We pledge to feed the green machine.

This green monster that is always hungry

Weds us as a patriotic bride on the winning team

If we stay loyal to the green machine.

The green monster is a maelstrom without a vortex.

Everything and Everyone lives in this green machine.

Even the poor are a number, a statistic

Feeding the machine that has eyes inside and out

Like satellites perched in heaven, shinning like a thief.

And, my accountant…he died April 15th.

Like Déjà vu

With hair to his shoulders

White shirt tucked into his blue jeans

Cigarette hanging from his lips

That cocky, cocky mannerism always breaking the ice

Seals his girlfriend's conviction to the rebellion.

He could not belong anywhere else in society

But to help generate the change.

Bare Bottom

Up is down

Down is up

He said, "OM."

Let us flip the murk

"Something stinks in Switzerland."

It smells like quarks!

COMBAT

Ramboon the buffoon

Rammed a ramrod

Up my pantaloon

Before he slit my throat

USA Guard

In the forest blacker

Than a moonless night

He is

Positioned

As a chess pawn.

It is an Icon

Keeping Peace.

Awaken

By the rising sun

Peaking

Through the thickness

Of the trees

He climbs

Down the tower.

His foot touches

Unblemished

White snow.

He remembers it is Christmas!

Generals will feed him cake.

5 Haiku Poems of Our Galaxy

Sagittarius

A* Heaven has memory

Fox jump quantum hole

        Slice of crescent moon

        Desert stars sing strong, sing loud

        Echo in black hole

A celestial

Body, brings its bright brilliance

On Oppenheimer

        Cosmic mystery

        Colors in our galaxy

        Blue laser focus

Sagittarius

A* Galactic conundrum

Such élan vital

The NIF Sepulcher

Timeless tolls take him into travels

Depths of the deep dark, the unknown

Deep into the unconscious vortex

Of the mind, here he abodes

Alone, being an inventor

The being, beginning, claims

 to be benign to humanity.

He is the gatekeeper to insanity.

The most insane song is past

Singing to future in one timpani.

He cries, I've got it!

Humbles his perception of power.

He life is on hold, and forgets

About his poverty, all poverty.

He is a man - an Adam of the Universe.

He holds the Universe

As if it were a baby

His arms cradle it, rocks it, coos it

In its dove innocence – the Universe.

He harnesses its wild nature

Yet has no crib to lay his broken body.

Captured in the turmoil of this status

He takes the staff of radiant laser light

Wants to slice clean through darkness – the unknown.

He lands on the street with two broken feet

Still claiming to be benign to humanity.

The only malignancy is claims is humility

The inventor holds the radian laser staff of sepulcher

Ready to ignite it whenever Freedom give him the GO!

Without Fear.

Meet Me Inside You

An outside world looks in at me.

I stay still, quiet as can be.

I do not hiss, nor shuffle, neither breath

Without exclusive rights to my life.

It is my life; merely their interpretation.

They look in at me uninvited.

The dust settles into stillness.

Let them interpret empty tumultuous space

Until they learn to look in at me

While looking in at themselves.

The rights cease to be exclusive

It is now common ground.

Strawberry Folk Poem

There was a farmer from Terre Haute

Whose name was Ziggy.

He discovered a solution which made

Strawberries real biggies.

The strawberries were so big

One supplied three months feed for a pig.

This made the Hoosier farmer

One happy Ziggy.

Ziggy ran to the White House

To tell his friend Buff.

Congressman Buff soon shut

Ziggy's ass up, and said

"Next time get a permit

Or, you'll see where you sit

Out on your duff, with no home

Now leave with that stuff!"

Ziggy knew that wasn't right

But he didn't want to fight.

So, he and the Mrs. laughed

While tasting giant strawberries each night.

The Flight Stops At Las Vegas

Going up, up, up and up

Mounds of ground grow smaller

Smaller, smaller as I stare

At growing cotton balls, they float

Magically. It is magic in the air.

I look through air portholes

At vast blue serene sky

Farms and fields are earth's blankets

Worn patterns wrap earth warmly

White and tan are saddles of sand

Beautiful, so bare

Sun is the great lantern

Illuminating his warm hue

Saluting us as we sink, descending

Low, low, lower

Sleepy eyes open

To the shock of bombs

It was not only neon

Waxed

Smell the rose bud

mmmmm…mmmmmm

Oh no! Let's scram!

Here come the nippers.

They'll clip it, dip it

And set it aside.

Not to hide it…you yoyo

To kill the scent.

Lady Liberty

No offense statue

But blaspheme and idolatry

Will always flatter

Without freedom

Changing the "N" word

As John Lennon, and Yoko said

"Woman is the n… of the world."

"She is the slaves of slaves."

Woman replies,

Pick me up in your nuclear coach

I do not care what color the horse is

White, red, black or gray

Since you will not allow me my own way.

For I think radioactive isotopes

Need to take an interplanetary trip

From Mother Earth to Father Sun

Where we no longer need to hide

That nasty stuff, otherwise, everyone

And everything is now "N…s"

Origin

Is she a man, or is she a woman?
Is she a woman by congenital origin?
She is a woman…but a man
Christ, who supped with her
She is a cornerstone.

Is he a man, or is he a woman?
Is he a man by congenital origin?
He is a man…but a woman
Who quickened his dead spirit
He is a last Adam.

Pink Capitalism

Syd made up a new language

Whereby all one needs to do is read the resonance.

Unfortunately, this type of reading takes

Special apparatuses, only available for order

Off dairy milk cartons, and no one drinks dairy

Any longer. The co-op of dairy farmers then

Bought the rights to these special glasses and

Started to distribute them on *Your Turn Website*

We all realize when we start to read this

New language the quick flash of flesh is

To keep us awake in our immunization to the

Social engineering *that having a job is the best*.

A quotation from the 1% desk.

Syd has us now reading government secrets.

But then a beer came out advertising even better

Glasses to read Syd's new language which reads

"Peace wants love," so we all join "3Floyds.com" instead.

Educated Weed Heads

Is Satan- the socialist to survive another season

The GOP ask, wearing their white wigs.

A socialist gathering started amongst

The Burn supporters…we decided the best

Of two evils is to listen to Karl Marx.

Who said "Got to have socialism

To have a true Democracy."

Something *The Burn* would say.

And his listeners would follow.

Makes sense to me. That way my neighbor

Would know what the hell

I was talking about

As we sat to share conversation.

My neighbor would have the

Prerequisites to know how to make a

Democracy.

Do not lose your job

The Los Angeles neighborhood is well lite by streetlights. I approach a home, knock on the door, a foreigner answer. The homeowner understands English completely; however, does not comprehend the meaning of freedom of speech. I ask this person to sign, the Comprehensive Test Ban Treaty petition. The homeowner replies in his paranoia, "leave it up to the government, it is the government's business; talk to the government."

I proceed to the next door. A University instructor working at UCLA answers. He is 100% in favor of the Comprehensive Test Ban Treaty. He would love to join our citizen lobby group; however, the only way he is able to keep his job and keep the funding going into the UCLA labs, is to work on the R&D for biochemical warfare. Therefore, he cannot sign our petition.

I knock on the next door. It is a contractor who tells me to get the "fuck" off his property. And, "if – America does not proceed on with our progress he claims, we will all end up like the people in India, or Ethiopia with nothing!" He throws his beer bottle at me. Which I dodge. Consequently, we move on to another neighborhood.

I knock on the next door…

The Cold Moon

The cold moon, the blood moon

the beginning of the cold war

Randy and I sit in his

red convertible, we call Redstone

Not like the missile, but red stone

like the natural red rock amphitheater

where the Grateful Dead played

against a cold moon, on 7-8-78

Randy and I watch the bold moon, the cold moon

the blood moon sits majestically

on our southwest desert Alamogordo

home of the Pershing missile

New Mexico, Alamogordo Our home

Our backs turned

to the Organ Mountain's eruption

we sit, stare at the desert

at the blood red moon, the cold moon

like it is an alien that has invaded our planet

It is 1945 New Year Trinity Ball dropping

We look deep into the red ball, blood moon to see if

there are tiny people inside, some survivors perhaps

It is the cold war in 1947; it is the next year marking

the end of the mortal life of Mahatma Gandhi

Had to be that way

to make room for the "paper clip" operation

coming in from Germany to Alamogordo New Mexico

Alamogordo retirement home of the "Fat Man"

Where visitors roll in on buses

gather inside a chain link fence

and stare at a once atomic, now mass of metal

sitting in the middle of the southwest desert

surrounded by chain link fence, like a monument

Yes, I will follow the Pershing missile to Germany

I will walk in a tunnel each day in my camouflage

protecting the Pershing missile

A musician pan handles in the same tunnel; it is his tunnel

Each day he plays, protesting the Pershing missile

with his music; it is the cold war 1982 in Germany

The bold cold moon and Pershing missiles perch in Germany

I walk through his tunnel as a visitor, hear his pan handling

I drop a US 5-dollar coin in the musician's hat

He looks up at me, with blood moon eyes

a look not of gratitude, but of compromise

Uranium Butterfly

Bare feet blister in hot cave

fumigated by uranium dust

where the old woman has no fire

to brew her tea.

Butterflies flutter from fields

fumigated by uranium dust

like quarks, they defy gravity.

Young man neglects his studies

on this day, to cut down last tree

growing in his ancient forest-

fuel for the old woman to brew.

Yet, the teenager has no fuel to listen

to Jim Morrison on the radio.

No laser ratification

neither motes, nor neutralization.

No nuclear neutralization.

ONLY ARMS PROLIFERATION!!!

No Neutralization of nuclear waste!

Young man makes a case

to harvest uranium fields, where

uranium butterflies flutter up, up, and up

like magical photons, ascending, ascending

ascending like Jesus Christ!!!

Where matter is incorruptible…

Seeing Fission in the Fog

The word fission can mean to split, divide, or cleave into parts. However, these descriptions are much to plain, and do not give justice to the power behind what fission is capable of.

Fission can be the wrath of man as in igniting an atomic bomb, powered by the explosion of man's ignorance. Or man can choose to utilize fission in a natural and graceful setting as a single living cell divides to become two new whole bodies.

However, man chooses to use it; it can ultimately mean a beginning, or it can mean an end. For we know God created fission, man merely discovered it on loan. How we choose to use this loan, will determine if we can pay the price.

LAMENTATION

The Key of David

Hear harps hallow in the wind
Harmonicas humming holy hymns
We gather, listening to tambourines jangle.
An audience runs to a mountain of sanctum.
Drums beat on the tympanum.
Raise arms and hail, the Root of David prevails
To open the white seal.
Within guitars' strings wrangle Heaven's riffs
Emotions wrung out, as the blood drips
Splattering onto unturned stones.

Drums beat fire, dead rise, leaving, leaving.
Harpers harp, singers sing, tambourines jangle
Flutes pipe upon mountains of sanctum.
The trumpets shout!
Open the white seal key of David
Call MUSIC
An invention of mankind
Created by the Master in his mind
Called GOD.
Wrung out emotions drip blood.

Short

The story is too, too long
Too long to tell.
How it begins?
I can't even begin.
Come to the point?
The view was changed
In the last days.

Over

Look…if you feel
Correction is backstabbing
You should have known
The Rules
Before playing ball.
Now try the curve over
Using honesty as the pitch.
The umpire is watching
His name is God.

Hitting Bottom

Yes, he remains changed

No, nothing appears the same

Since he dove, touched bottom

Before coming up.

Do you know

What I am talking about?

Have you been there?

I ask

Have you been to the

Bottom of the pit?

Or are you still there?

Hel…Ms

Wil…Son

Come out of the pit?

All Sons do.

Rays

Feel the hot sun's rays as you wade in the stream.

Race on to the sandy bank, before the tide increase.

Let the rays dry you while you rest. Fall asleep.

Dream, dream, dream on dreamer

Of nature's tomorrows

Of high intensity laser beams

To work on my teeth. Zap, wow, ok.

Do you think Orion and Pleiades care

To have a dental work over today?

Wake up! Where are the hot sun's rays?

Where is the sun?

Where are Orion and Pleiades?

Where?

For sins have reached the Heavens

Say it the Lord, Wow!

Two Xmas Poems for "KLSX" Los Angeles

Poem#1

In one year

One month

A day

And an hour

My true love

Gave to me

A pain

In the butt!

Poem #2

An angel who did not know here she was headed

Was hit by a ton of bricks; she squeaked to the bunch

Of angels who knew not where they were headed

 nor cared. They squeaked to the angel buried alive

Asked her if they may take the bricks home

To build a bookshelf. She answered

Just take these damn things off me

I feel as if I am in Beirut

And should had left early with the guy

Who went out for that glass of water.

Conceit

Don't place me high
Upon a pedestal.
Don't idolize me.
Don't treat me as if
As if I were a god.

"Are you nuts? I don't!"

Oh…
You mean it's me?

"Yup."

Diomedes

Agamemnon's reign of power

Achilles outrage of pride

Patroclus' mistaken identity

Hector's wholeness, "breaker of horses"

With wife at his side.

But Diomedes

Oh Diomedes

Once, Faith in God!

Now turn to War Cry!

Oh Diomedes

Little brother

Stand up against the

Final woe

Come under the altar

My little tribulation saints

C O R N E R S T O N E

Is it caused by chance this contact
For our hearts hunger to hear
A name so proper for the founder
That cornerstone twangs in our ears?

Neither by chance nor coincidence
Nor by the providence of God
It is predestination written
By the Omnipotent rod.

Are trances of climactic elation
Thrown to us by destiny
That we will sing with fervor
A song of pure clemency?

A bright light comes, carrying those
Above God's first and second ceiling
To reveal no experience can humble as can
First the Word, then Faith, and last Feeling.

Is it the voice behind the movement

Which roars to us as a Lion

That quickens our lost souls

Or do we merely hear Earth crying?

It is shown by Edwards, that sixty-nine times seven

Passed of Daniel's Apocalyptic vision

So that the purged Riders

Will forever carry on, without remission.

Tell us time then it is true

The trumpets sounding are not mere

Emotions you do capture

But truly the anointed Bride

He- Jesus did rapture.

Know this by Faith, the time is always at hand.

Revelation comes not in one man's interpretation.

And, New Jerusalem, she comes

As a NAKED LAND.

Sally Child

(sonnet for children)

The drum does pound, as every penny drops
To tell Salvation Army children cheer!
For the day may come, when you do turn five
A seed for you, will be awaiting there.
A seed to cherish, for it brings you life
The faith in Christ Jesus and a prayer.
As the Church is, you are a blessed bride
The wedding the climb up on Heaven's stair.
A gift that is not earned, but gave by Grace
To kids with faith in Jesus and a prayer.
When wicked war takes your house to the ground
It leaves you without, as so with it all
You must learn to part, but one will remain
The seed of Jesus inside you: your heart.

I CAN SEE

I see God's voices
I see the trumpets sounding
While reading my braille.

A Dream Call

In dream, the child inside tunnel's narrow passage

One end meets day. His feet hold fast this edge.

Begins the vastness of fields, empty. He sees no one.

At far meadow he stares, in solitude still at edge

Of day. Then he turns to face the deepness of tunnel.

Sees darkness face to face. Walls for protection blind

Both sides of him. Far from this is another end of passage.

Two ends revealed, one Death, the other Life.

His back is turned on day, he begins to walk in darkness.

Keeping sight of a narrow hole. The dream travels

Well pass entry of the night, and darkness soon passes

On to light. It is vast! Thousands, and thousands

All poised in place. Light before him, this must be God!

He looks at line that travels through this timeless Heaven.

God's creatures ride this line. They smile on the child

Singing as they pass him. Leap on their music sings.

Heaven now, no need to wait, but wait a voice tells him

Leap not for this line will not vanish. But once on

You are not, no coming back, so child come slowly to the

End and leap not. He goes back through the darkness back

To the edge of day where the meadow grows dark

Darker. He sings to the meadow which blossom to

Sing with him, darkness you must have to see God's day.

VANITY

(Pope John Paul II lacks)

Spirits which corrupt us, come to us

It is we who set them ablaze

Until our eyes can see.

We put them into perdition.

We are the White Fire

The White Spirit

The only Flesh saved.

We have the keys

To Heaven and Hell

And we live both

Justified

Not by our own will.

Who is the Divine one?

A   GALLOP

From the third unknown heaven so sounds
The one white call, a rider's crux cry.
And upon the green young unseen valleys
He gallops where blades rise alive.
While the grass not passé rubs
Their elbows the music arrives, a song new
None can learn but those who survive.

And the seal it is broken to new
Age rhyme, clearing the air
Of enigmas of Baals' last chime.
And the arrow does shoot with one bow
For the straight narrow target – a
Kindred be bound to one mind.

And so, spirits are quickened to see
Revelation – the seeds they do sow
It is music of holy derive
Where emotions will dictate
Without the perception of time
It is the only, from third unknown heaven
Gallop to arrive, to the peculiar.

LOVE

Love's Locked Door

I.

What may my heart expect this autumn night?

Oh, quickened winds blow silver clouds home.

Sing love in flight. For solitude I divest.

For laughter cries unilaterally.

And numbness amplifies as I still search.

The instincts become keen to overreach.

But oh, one cloud draws near, never brighter!

I am Jonas, and love he reaches swiftly

When with sword. Bravely out from the serpent's

Clutch, love saves me, in Heaven kisses me.

Two young pigeons make one bed.

Two melodies become one when the song

Is the same within each pigeon's head.

Love draws strong when captured in a single song.

II.

The bitter cold on a winter night bites.

While flames of fire burn all in sight.

The fire burns a devil's red bed.

I am Jonas, saved from the past cold lays

Made for poor eyes, the lustful, the loveless, the dead.

Love's imaginary touch still scorches

My flesh. And the true thorn reveled, the curse

No gentleman's manners, flesh in his eyes

A man's soul is rich, yet still insatiable.

Two turtle doves are thrown into the fire

One made to be a sacrifice for sin

The other, a burnt offering, both are killed

At the temple door for their desire.

Love burns strong, when it cries in arms we belong.

III.

Oh, the fever that festers in the spring
The flute that blows a tune, silk sheets are laid
For you, black stains, white plague, a witch's brew
Flutes never blow to blue. I am Jonas
Caught between two truths, what is and what seems
Love looks into the mouth of the serpent.
Comes out laughing at himself: it is for fools.
Two black ravens are at the door crying.
How long, how long, must we be strong?
If no angel be given in marriage
The warmth of the sun then, as long been gone.
We fear that our feathers flutter without
Feeling anymore. Love festers from fear of not.
Love is forlorn Lord. Bitter waits are long.

IV.

Under a watchman's tower summer tells

A tale, love remains well, it reads clearly.

I am Jonas, but love raises my soul

Quickly, as I see his soul against those

Souls of mediocrity. Thus devotion

Saves me, as I hold his rarity dearly.

Hungry hearts bleed; there are many. But the man

The woman will bestow lordship to, hides

His fortitude in humble honor.

And her femininity like a shadow

Seals his insecurity. Two sea mews

Make for the shore, leaving sorrows forevermore

Leaving the world to sulk in its mockery.

When worn long, love lingers in the same song.

V.

What may my heart expect this autumn night?
Heavy rains will not refrain from purging
What is not yet tame. My Anti-Aesthetic
Garment spews out the hieratic priest.
For Michael stands in the river between
Two olive trees, whose roots draw libido
Stronger than Daphne's laurels Apollo wore
As piercing as Caesar's crown which drew blood.
Rain will never hit harder, for our times
Sees hate come closer, while love grows farther.
The days are Jonas'. Love is doomed to explore.
Holy white doves set up desolation
Unable to pierce their mate's isolation.
Their hearts' higher loyalty, He hides the key.

Hallow Hope

A half-moon sets on this twilight.

The stars sparkle not so bright.

Tonight, spread across a mediocre

Dark sky, it is not too cold

An evening, for an almost winter night.

The scent of salt, is it still there?

My face remains sprayed by sea air.

In the quiet twilight

I hear that hornpipe hallow

In a holy ghostly wind.

Look that sailor has come home!

Or, maybe that was years ago.

My memory has an omission.

I remember the sea swallowed

That sailor, not too long ago.

A half-moon sets on this twilight.

Sea, spew that sailor back to me

When you are through thrashing him.

It is not too dark a night, and

The lighthouse dimly shines on.

Paper Pick-Up

Sis, I showed a guy a poem today.

"What did he say?"

Don't waste it on paper, baby.

"Well, were you horney

Or was the poem horney?"

Neither.

"He must have been."

Jealousy

Never, never, never hurt

I am home. When will good-by be gone?

When will you be home?

Why do you go out?

When you are out

Don't do it

With another

When you are gone.

Assumption

Oh dear, the sin stains my soul.

But let me ask you brother

Did you ever want someone

So bad, so very bad, that

You were afraid to receive

Him or Her?

You were frightened that

Perhaps, reality

Is not quite what your mind

Made him or her out to be.

So, you convince yourself, yes

Reality must be, better

And you travel towards that

Which your mind has you believing

You cannot live without.

And you leave one for another.

Oh dear, saying sorry will never, never

Release that sorrow

That has already afflicted

You and me, forever.

Your sorrow is loss of me

My sorrow is sin stains my soul.

But regardless of that

I walk out your door

Into a limbo.

Out yours and yet not

Into the other

For it was shut

A minor detail I overlooked

Oh, dear me.

ONE   MAN

I   AM

AN   ADDICT

I   AM

ADDICTED

AN   ADDICT

AN ADDICTION

TO   A MAN

TO ONE MAN

THAT   IS   IT

A   L   L

O   N   E

T O   A

S I N G L E

M   A   N

T H A T ' S

O   N   E

T H A T ' S

A   L   L

O   N   E

M   A   N

Wishing Well

Long ago she made a wish that mounds of men

Would woo her, war for her, want her kiss.

Long ago she made a wish, red rose never

Ceased to arrive upon her silver dish.

Men would ravish her; this was her wish.

Long ago he made a wish, moments he sat on top

Of the world with his friends were endless.

They would laugh, they would look down on it

The world to mock it. To sit with friends

On top of the world to watch it, this was his wish.

Long ago she came upon that wishing well and sat by it.

Long ago he found her there, and by her he did sit.

They fell in love, deep and quick, words would not

Reveal how they felt, at that wishing well.

And so, they stood up and looked into the well

To make another wish, that is, to know each other's kiss.

But before they could they both fell into the well

Without their second wish.

By many other suitors was she forever ravished.

Endlessly he stayed with his friends

On top of the world as they all mocked it

Both without relief.

Babies Given Up

Bosoms cry for babies
She gives suck in final days
The time is given up
It is for and to sweet savior
Have mercy, look beyond action, have mercy

Babies dry from lack of natural mother's arms
Day care centers are a home
Abortion clinics is where they go
The psychiatrist is a good friend
Housekeepers she lives in
Have mercy, the time is given up, have mercy

The world takes, the water swallows.
The babies dry, the bosoms cry
Bosoms cry for natural babies…Mother Earth.
Pray it is not a pig who receives suck
When Mother Earth gives milk.

WET

Rain ran down the drain
Guided by the steady flow
Of the wet, which came.
Being drenched is a drag.
I must dry off.
Please, hand me a rag.

A Fling

We kick orange leaves
His arm around my shoulder
My name is not Lynn!!!

A Flash of Guilt

I wonder
What it is like
Brushing my fingertips
On your chest
While we gaze into each other's eyes.

You fondle the nipple
Of my breast.
Your hand moves slowly
Down my stomach
And, lower.

My hand moves up
Caressing your neck
And higher.
Gently my fingers
Bury in your hair.

Drawing your head
To my breast.
Your lips kiss my body
Move up
Higher up my neck

Both your hands move abruptly
Clenching my hair.
Your body with one quick bounce
Blankets over my body
We stare.

Into the deep
Each other's eyes.
Your face draws
Towards mine.
Both faces are
Consumed in fire.

You lay your lips on mine.
And, I feel more than just
Your tongue
Enter my body.
In the heat of passion
During a quick breath
I ask myself…Lord
Did you release me from the label
Adulteress?

Dear Mr. Woznicki

The night crept on, drawn long
When alone, in the night
Without a home, cold and alone
A creature crushed to the bone
Wounded by Christ who awakens
The sparrow with clipped wings
Struggling to fly into tomorrow
Refugee in her own native land
She is a wounded lamb
For came a manifest destiny
Ignorant, polluted her sand
Prostituted her land
Denied common welfare for gain
Manhood compensating in every way
For long the sparrow awaits alone.

She saw him, but he saw her first
His gallant eyes kissed her gaze
Thoughtful compassion on his face
The voice sunk deep into her relief
He said come home with me into safety.
His invitation more precious than a jewel
Thus, it was Chivalry that night who ruled.

Chivalry was his name who gave

Sparrow a branch to lay

Her head, while keeping her skirt on

The sparrow asks what I may do to repay you

Chivalry claimed, long ago I met an acquaintance

Samaritan was his name; he took me in just the same

Under the same roof they did lay

Chivalry and sparrow day after day

Their friendship grew and grew

Respect protected the two

He lay his head upon her breast

In pure and loving friendship

Sparrow flew on into tomorrow

Chivalry had no sorrow

For both returned to rest

Upon the highest nest

Christ had prepared

THREE LOVE POEMS

Clogged

Not being able to think clearly

Because that other person has

Clogged your line.

Prayer

A young girl placed a letter

Inside the Bible

Addressing it to God

Asking Him for a perfect mate.

A woman realized He answered.

Fundamental Burning Piece

I'd like to wrap my

"Whom He called He justified,"

Legs around your neck

Smoking Musician

Michael moves in mandolin twilight

writing spontaneous lyrics to his master-

Moon of love, of lust, of luck, of locomotion

Michael is a bold fisherman hitting on big rhymes

leans over to kiss the girls; catches them every time

Michael sings in the moon's musical twilight

and he hums Rastafarian rhymes

Awarded. His moon light music came

before the mainland knew what ganja meant

D.C. celebrates the musician the most authentic brand.

Dense green smoke lingers in his familiar aura

lingers longer than the heavy London fog he frequents

And, our liberal leaders like him for more

than just his songs, but for his peace pipe too

Michael watches waves kiss the moon lit horizon

Waves roll in florescent flashes of ah

He hums hard explosive vibrations of feelings, singing

to a woman who interprets his heart-rending expressions

as direct exchange to her exposed hunger, exclusively

She falls into an intoxicated love spell

Michael knows how to make a move to the mandolin moon

Me, My Mirror, And the Moon.

My mirror is on the moon

Mirror, mirror on the moon

who is to blame, for all my doom

my mother, my father

the social injustice

my brother, my sister

my preacher, my friend

my doctor, my neighbor

my teacher, say again

my butcher, my baker

my police down the street

some call a hater

my God, my religion

my mentor who claims

he has apocalyptic visons

I feel the same

Mirror, mirror on the moon

who is to blame, for all my doom, reflecting at me

Mikhail's Moon

I flew to the moon with Mikhail Gorbachev

on Virgin Airlines, we went to put a rose

on *The Little Prince's* grave

I flew to the moon with Mikhail Gorbachev

on Virgin Airlines, we went to put a lantern

on Ronald Regan's grave

I flew to the moon with Mikhail Gorbachev

on Virgin Airlines, we went to put popcorn

on Teddy Kennedy's grave

Mikhail Gorbachev stakes his claim

It is now Mikhail's Moon, Mikhail and I sit on his moon

watching Star Wars, eating popcorn, by the light of the

lantern and the fragrance of the friendship rose

All the while Putin and The Pope are in Budapest

Wolfkins

The Town quiet in routine

unknowing of an undercurrent

leaking seepage of steam

through cracks in the ground

The Town goes on each day wondering why

the wind blows ominous clouds by

hearing the howling of a hound

never feeling the full moon

or the need to moon-walk

to transfer out of body

like weird wolves hoping to manifest

The Town quiet in routine

does not recognize a dog trot transportation

taking place on the sidewalk

in front of their inert homes

It is difficult to imagine life

without maenads; they chase after

Dionysus in their frenzy groupieness

disguised in graceful bones

They are caught up, in the chorus line

of cords, picking on change

breaking sound barriers of behavior in time

Like a cancer they cling on Dionysus

whenever they feel the world wrapping

those in hedonistic habits like

having the time to moon-walk

The Town quietly worries, unwilling to commit

to involvement, walk upon the same cement

mind boggled, how it even came to be

the cracks on the ground

or the voluptuous moon

In the havoc or right and left

black or white, truth or lie, I

remain a maenad…you a Dionysus

We draw up each crack until

it is solid foundation to moonwalk

without stubbing our toe

Once children controlled by

social consumption we disrobe

leaving it laying on the street

we re-robe wearing only the cracks

from the ground too proud

for parental guidance

We moonwalk throwing the ball

of change back and forth to one another

leaving each other standing every time

vertical with the moon in our veins

hoping to repaint the world

concave, instead of leaving it convex

Eric

On the gay rides

The hay rides

The last day of the

World Fair, in San Francisco

Where the statue of Liberty has

Beauteous breast, and a dick

We remember her heart and love her.

Save Me

His love a trillion stars in twinkle's glance

A billion grains of sand in hourglass

A million waltzes winnowing in grass

A thousand sharp arrows, a narrow pass

Forever steward sups with love complete

With me in this narrow shallow sin sea.

WOMB

Water, warm in womb, a private tomb

Sacred, but not to acids and sulfates

Womb without breath, organically I too die

In that moment too late, when the wave tunnels

As a mother's womb, only to erupt

As a Sperm Whale's spout spews out that spark

Of Life- made in that moment, in an iota of love

Little withered heart, and little withered feet

I am a silent forest

A faint beneficiary of Faith

That the womb does not stay barren

Only in hibernation until the next sowing

Until the next seed, until the next harvest

Reparation

Awaken the grave at Al-Awja, exhume the soul

The trial is not over, voices are in vaults

Written from caves, shipped to trusted sorter.

Keeper of handwritten words, upon frayed cloth

America the Beautiful, forever freedom

What says the voices?

Who cry Anfal, who cry Halabja?

Pull the ghost out to stand trial, for no denial

Iraqi state files, spell GENOCIDE.

Al-mukharrebin sabotage Satan's soul

Fly your own freedom flag as Peshmerga

Return only to rank of Kurdistan

Ranya rise as phoenix for reparation is due

And the World Court died long, long ago inside

Inside its Peace Palace.

Ode to My Bra

God have mercy, for All land is God's acre.

The acre is but a burial ground, not our home.

It is not the orange orchards in spring blossoms

Where Santa Paula's singing, playing children roam.

It is a babbling Babylon of Babel, done by the devil's bell.

It is no longer the gate of God, but the gate to hell.

It is a land before the United Nations, without recognition.

A land infested by men to be revealed as sons of Perdition.

God have mercy, brand us bold, hard as a stone.

Give us faith to bury the lost in his pit

Where his flesh rot to the bone.

You shut the door leaving us alone, in the room

Where the living Lion lives; if our faith famishes

Would be our doom. So, make us proud to be peculiar

And happy at heart, for our new eyes have sight to see far.

Blow in powers of righteous Spirits; surround empiric darkness

For we must, burn his black cloth until his flesh is but dust.

Draw the lines, and mark the borders

brings back Mesopotamia as a land or order.

Allow the land to vomit out the sons of perdition

Those inhabitants who murder

Clear waters of Tigris and Euphrates

Give Drink to my destitute brother

Remove the wicked, for there is no place

For a Herod Antipas. I pray my bother hold fast.

Land of my brother's the borders are secured by daughters

And the white dove sits as the right hand, of Kurdistan.

Love for the Homeless

I do not care about the shape you're in

If you lay around all day, and all night

I do not care if you never get off

The ground to fight

It is alright if all you want to do

Is to shine your light

I don't care if people say you're strange

If they make you beg, and laugh your way

I do not care if you are on a binge

You abuse 8 balls and now you crawl

I do not care if people see your face

Then run the other way in disgrace

For it's said the poor will always be

So, you stay in that tent under that tree

A Veteran

He takes a steer by the horn

He takes soy instead of pig rind

He's no longer much for working

But he offers help, and is always kind

He eats tofu in the morning

And in the evening, he drinks

Barley over wine

His hair may be purple

And braided all in a twine

Unable to get a hair cut

It is the least on his mind

He always salutes the day

With his hair purple

All twined in a braid

You may see him waving

His little American Flag

Wearing his purple heart

While you are at the parade.

Borderline

Peko rode on a freight train over the borderline.

He claims to the parole he has never committed a crime.

But posse are always one step behind

When Peko comes to America to earn a dime.

The mayor takes Peko's money, and leaves Peko in a bind

Made Peko take that freight train, back over the borderline

Peko never carried a Smith and Wesson

Only his umbrella and his English lesson

Which Mrs. Smith had given to him

For pruning her roses, which is her deepest passion.

Where Loyalty Lies

In the deep, lies a land called chaos

Where Sigmund toiled over the hands

Which brought the death of Laius

Sophocles used the female

As the lever, luring lust inside

The deep chaos, where Sigmund

Toiled over the clever, child of libido.

For Oedipus was so clever he became the Rex

Loved his mother to his blindness, and to her death.

But the question has always been about the CROSSROAD.

Does it really matter which way we go?

Or are me doom by predestination

To only learn the truth too late.

That Mother and Child is a holy fate.

Time

He turned back the clock to stop time

To give us an interlude

An intervention for the prevention

Of the human crime

of killing off civilization

With ignorant neglect

While we sublime ourselves.

THE KINDRED DINER

It is difficult to determine the walls were made of aromatic pine

Oiled and fresh at one time, now handwritten names

One-dollar bills, postcards, photos, and torn pages

from magazines told us the diner was once a logging mill

We sat in chairs where the tables had small brass plaques

Informing us that the furnishings had come off

Old Queen Mary Jane, which the public had thought

Sunk off the shores of Cape Hope during a crash.

With the Coast Guards touring the Peruvian Highlands.

The diner floors were made of cobblestone

Giving the guest the impression, the outside was in

And the inside gave us the believe we were out

With skylight windows above us, and star all about.

A large sign hung above the antique Columbian cash register

Which read: We reserve the right to refuse service

To anyone famished of faith; we don't feed the dead.

Friends

Green waves great crash over thee

Fear not through the darkness of the night

His eyes will guide you where no starts are in sight

For ominous clouds pass over, their right to shine.

He will plot your course through uncharted time

Be not famished of faith my friend, it's not the end.

As your vessel moves forward believing it safe

A whale bellow's its strength upside your starboard, shake

Safety over until your vessel breaks

He is your raft, let loneliness in deep water pass

Be not famished of faith my friend, it's not the end.

Darkness still upon you, but your heart is relieved

For now, your feet feel sand, as you pass over your grief

Savage sharks start to attack you as you touch the sand

He is your life jacket, reach out to Him with your hand

Be not famished of faith my friend, it's not the end

Lay on the shore, allow the lacerations to leak

The last drops of your sorrow, for in this night's storm

It is not your grief you shared, but He did borrow

Little worried

If ever they saw each other again

About being attractive to one another

Superficiality

Caught up in cloud

"The church got caught up in the air"

Evening News at Dinner

will he be the supernova

that collapses in society's lap

he promises to be blue skies, forever

and battle ground is not in the Middle East

and battle ground is not on Capitol Hill

and battle ground is not *CNN* and *Fox*

he promises rainbows and sunset horizons

but the news dissipates into the dew

for me and for you by next morning

this is not a fantasy; nor false news

listen to his lips on the TV tube

the words coming off that TV tube

which we hear clearly are true

"it is not what he eats that defiles him

it is what comes out of his mouth that defiles him"

unfortunately, every time he opens his mouth

he is real news, ugh

Bake the Cake

Taking in a stranger is sometimes

The only rescue, to bring your own salvation.

Big Brother feeding the hunger of the homeless

Feeds his hunger of giving out his love.

Continue to feel at place with your peers.

Do not remove the cake before it is finished to bake.

Fix it with stevia and put in your higher thoughts.

Make sure the world honors you with your fate.

Turn street bums into musical magic, and aesthetic art.

Turn a generation into a revolutionary cause.

Do your wizard's wonderful wand whirling with wild wind

Without taking a pause, generation to generation to generation.

For we can not get the ingredients back again.

So, bake that cake, wholesome and good, lasting.

Cross

She found one drop of blood

In El Salvador

It was a USA Republican current

Full of bananas

Festering war

In the green fields where

Children's voices tore

Out the page **13**

Not

The river raged green waters

Over solid rocks

As pillars of solitude

They budge not

Statues of isolation

The rocks grew from the ground

With grudges hidden by

the raging waters sound

If he would know me

I would not be alone

For my door is always open

Inside he would have found

A love so deeply grounded

It could not be moved

By raging waters

Nor by his solitude

Wilderness

In untamed wilderness

Of my mind

Where cigarettes and alcohol

Knock habitually

On the impulsive urges

Lingering

Admission and abstaining

A beautiful recovery

One day, at a time

Humbleness

To human weakness

As if it were "a thorn

On my side"

Gender

Macho maniacs

Fancy frills

Iron clamoring

Female fraternities

Drummers drills

Masculine, Feminine, or Neutral

Individuality still

Holds up in heaven

And eager to come out.

Individuality

Come out of the closet

Not as an equal.

Individuality

Come out of the closet

As highest-ranking existence.

On a Dove's Tuesday

Wind spread road as far as it can go

Scattered into an unrecognizable dust bowl

Foundation is formlessness now

Not even an iota of truth is left

Of Middle America

Where have you gone

Backbone

The graying nonconformist

Like an economic beast

Is here in full force

To create an élan vital for

The masses of six generations

Alive to vote, at the voting poles

Can save the untraveled road

To excitement and a new path

Forgive

Lay your ore in the rushing waters
Of this raging river of life, of love.
Find your own peace in this
New red, white and blue canvass.
Find order in all annulments to
Persecutors, intruders, and judgements.
For in our heavy fog of confusion
Love rings her bell loud and clear
Even your neighbor can hear
How well you forgive.

Eleanor's Rebuttal

Nothing more, Nothing more
Nothing more, Nothing more
I just want you to rap
Rap upon my door.

RAPTURE NEVER DIVIDED
PEACE

The 60's is underground.
Did the Elders eat up all the pie?
Or is there a piece left?
If so, give it to *The Burn*

About Author

"Norma Mahns was part of the thriving 1988-1993 Chicago poetry scene where the open mics around Wicker Park often heard her words," says C.J.Laity (Author or *Point Nemo*) of Chicago. Some of her published works include: "WOLFKINS" and "The Sepulcher," published in the *The Lumpen Times* 1993, Chicago Illinois USA. "The Cold Moon," is published in Chicago Poetry Press' anthology, *Journal of Modern Poetry 20*: The Poetry Writer's Guide to the Galaxy, April 2017. This collection includes Norma's first chap book, Paper Plague, is a collection of spiritual idiosyncratic poems, first printed in Los Angeles California 1988. It was later again reprinted by Society for the Prevention of Irreversible Catastrophe on Earth (S.P.I.C.E) Press, 1989 Chicago, IL. This is the first time Paper Plague is published. Many of Norma's poems include politics; for Norma has held a few activist positions and will always be an activist at heart. As a young teenager, she worked a summer for a California Alderman, Tom Haden, in a 1974 campaign to promote solar energy. In 1987 thru 1992 she was a staffed employee for the citizen lobby group - "For a Sane Nuclear Policy," also popularly known as SANE/FREEZE, or "The Freeze." She has stayed active in politics as a voting citizen who writes to her Representatives, Senators, and President. Norma Mahns served honorably in the United States Army as a still photographer. Currently she is retired from a civil servant position with the United States Federal Government. Norma studied poetry at Ventura College,

California; at Aurora College, Colorado; New Mexico State University, New Mexico; and Fayetteville University, North Carolina. She holds a bachelor's degree in management from National American University (NAU).

Norma Mahns

NOT THE END